Bad At Existing

Also by Madisen Kuhn

Almost Home
Please Don't Go Before I Get Better
Eighteen Years

bad at existing

MADISEN KUHN

madisen.co

FIRST EDITION — October 2022

Cover illustration and hand lettering by Leah Lu
Cover and interior design by Madisen Kuhn

ISBN 979-8-842601-95-0

For the ones who understand.

Content Warning

This book contains explicit language and poems that reference anxiety, depression, obsessive-compulsive disorder, trauma, abuse, sexual assault, grooming, self-harm, violence, death, and other potentially triggering material. Readers who may be sensitive to these themes, please take note. Your well-being is most important.

Contents

Coda

Author's Note

You know the feeling of waiting for something?

It sits low in your chest, alternating between melancholy and possibility, like lying down on a grassy hill, where time seems both static and too heavy.

I spent countless days as a twenty-three-year-old writing by the lake, waiting for my life to un-pause. I would tell myself I'd only be there for a little while but always left with sunburned shoulders. New freckles appeared across my nose, and the color in my cheeks made me look more alive than I felt. I carried a tick home on my right forearm, and the wound swelled for months. There's still a scar.

That summer, I learned that waiting feels a lot like hope.

But sometimes I worry that I will be waiting forever.

Waiting for my fears to quell, my wounds to heal, and the storm to pass. Waiting to wake up. Waiting to be real.

Waiting to become a better version of myself. The one who reads a massive stack of books each year. Who wakes up with the sun and hums while making breakfast in the kitchen. She wears her hair in braids and moves slowly through the supermarket aisles, closely inspecting apples for bruises in the produce section. She goes for long walks with only her thoughts. She's the friend you call when you need someone to help carry the heaviness of being human. She is good at existing.

I tell myself, "*one day, it will be easy to get out of bed*," but I am married to the man I've written poems about since I was eighteen. I have a home that is safe and comfortable. I have three dogs. I have so much of what I always wanted. And still, I find it hard to pull off the covers. I lie awake at night like the teenager who could not see the awakening on the other side of a nightmare. I was supposed to be better by now.

I've found that if I always look ahead to what's next, I can excuse myself from the present. I do not have to claim it. I can hide behind my intentions rather than hold hands with reality. I can withdraw, stepping back into the bushes until they swallow me.

Much of waiting is spent yearning.

I wish I lived somewhere else. I wish I was someone else. I wish I could fast-forward. I wish I never let myself get this bad.

But my hands cannot reach back to adjust the past or into the future to arrange what is to come. So, I freeze. I grow silent. Stuck inside my head. Obsessing over what could be. I close my eyes and wait to see what will happen.

When I deliberately pause to inspect my life, I see that the phases characterized by waiting held more complexity than was evident at the time. I recognize, in so many poems, that I was not waiting at all. Instead, I was uprooting myself to begin again. I was healing. I was slowly twisting out of old ways and preparing for newness. I was uncovering revelations and becoming intimate with my wants and fears. I cleared the table to make room for something different and often better.

It's lovely to dream. To write down ambitions in cursive, to pin photos of rooms and clothes I hope to find myself in someday. To believe in better. When I envision my idealized self, I hear birds singing. I hear the wind blowing through the trees. I see myself surrounded by beautiful things, warmth radiating from me like a golden aura. I feel at home in the world.

I think I'll always be waiting for something. For the burning yellow sunlight to wake me up. For the cold rain to wash away the layers of hurt and dust resting on the surface of my softness. For winter to pass. Waiting for tomorrow. Waiting to be whole. But I must cling to things that will remind me to not step out of my life while I wait for the next chapter. I must remind myself to not get lost in the longing.

What I am most often waiting for is myself. To get out of bed, to take the first step, to try. To open my eyes to what is already in front of me. To remember—

I exist to do more than simply pass the time.

Prelude

SECLUDED

I try to keep my brokenness a secret
It is easier to be broken alone

TENDER

I woke up and forgot it was October
On the front steps, I shook a little less
Than the last time we decided to rush
A season, shaking branches and wearing
Sweaters with the sun beating down
Tomorrow, it still won't feel like home
But I am learning that nothing does
Except for autumn and that first cool morning
Where the air smells like it did when I was ten
Before I knew that life would ever feel as unreal
As it does now, standing on one side of a door
Stirring up the courage to pull it shut

SUBMERGED

I would like to
be able to
feel something
without it
feeling like
the end of the
world

i only want to
stay when i know
it's time to go

RED MAPLE

The first days of fall are always warmer than I remember.
It just takes one cold morning to make me covet the glare.
Now I'm looking for any reason to go outside before dusk
begins to swallow our afternoons. I'm checking the mail on
a Sunday. I'm carrying a broken lamp to the shed. I don't
miss July and its quiet seethe. I miss the beginning. I miss
not knowing when it would end. It's a slice of sponge cake,
a half-erased underline left behind in a book that I can't
put down. I go inside and read it until the page corners
begin to curl. My nails were made for digging into palms.
I only want to stay when I know it's time to go.

I CARRY IT
ALL WITH ME
I HAVE NOT
FORGOTTEN

OTHERWORLD

I promise you, this is not the only life I've lived
There are otherworldly mirrors facing each other
That I've twirled divinely in between
Falling into the arms of dozens upon dozens
Of different reflections
I have breathed in their varying degrees of softness
Of heat
I whisper my secrets into each of their ears
Sit patiently as they whisper theirs back
I have loved and adored and obsessed and settled
More than this
Thousands of limbs covered in reddish purple memories
Cracking and growing with every beginning and end
When all I can do here is offer a passing smile
A near encounter
A faint aching of what could be
Know that I have loved you elsewhere
As I walk to the corner store, as I sit alone in my room
As the day fades into dusk
I carry it all with me. I have not forgotten

wasn't this
all supposed to be
beautiful
wasn't i supposed
to be free

THE MOMENT BEFORE SUNRISE

Life is composed of open ends, but I feel like it's closing in on me. Somehow, I have turned mine into an ongoing manhunt of myself, in which discomfort and unlikely tragedy chases me throughout all hours of the day. It never catches me, and yet, shallow breath catches in my throat, my tonsils swell like raw dough in the oven, no one will be there to kiss me goodbye. So I weep. I pace the wooden floor. I tear at my own skin like unbalanced kittens on a scratching post. Wasn't this all supposed to be beautiful. Wasn't I supposed to be free. Didn't I promise myself that I'd never get stuck. I wanted to be good at being alone. I wanted to be the sun. Instead, I hide from myself. I wish I could remember what certainty tastes like. But I am afraid of turning red. Or blue. Or bitter. Really, I am afraid of it all. Of never crawling out of the nightmare. Of dying before I tell the truth. Of considering who I might have been had I not decided I was fated to dissolve without the guiding hands of someone who surely knows better.

my whole life
i have been
looking for myself
in the gaze
of someone else

TULIP

My whole life
I have been looking
For myself in the
Gaze of someone else

I wonder what would
Happen if I never cut
My hair again
Or if I walked into the
Woods and never looked back

When I was a little girl
You told me that vampires couldn't see
Their own reflections

Every day I run
My tongue over the
Sharp points of my teeth
Burning to forget
The taste of strangers' wrists

I think I'll
stare out the
window forever
I think I'll never
grow tired
of the echo

THE PATRON SAINT OF POETS

What is something insignificant
That attaches itself easily to whatever
It picks up in the passing wind
Maybe a mosquito
I know people like to say their blood is sweet
They like to think of themselves as beloved
But the truth is you were only nearby
With a bit of leg to bite down on
They'll fill themselves up with
Anyone who gets close enough
I think I'm the same way or at least
I used to be
I could tell you why I tend to feel
So desperate for wholeness
Dressed up every morning in my black gown and veil
A hand-me-down rosary wrapped around my knuckles
But the story gets old the older I get
When I was little I told myself I'd never be
The dad in the sports car who only listens to oldies
But I've been practicing with the sound of rain
Held by the way it always comes down the same
I think I'll stare out the window forever
I think I'll never grow tired of the echo

i think i am
better at surviving
than i am
at living

HOURGLASS

I wonder if I would have gotten more done by now if it weren't for all the years I spent carving my initials into the trunk of a willow tree with a number two pencil. Would I have fallen asleep faster if the rivers weren't so dark. It's easier for me to pick at the lock when it's raining and yet like a small dog I curl into myself at the quiver of thunder. I remember my youth pastor in the cramped attic of a Southern Baptist church one night explain that there are two types of people—those who pray when things are good and those who pray when things are bad. I wonder if it is okay to love something only when you are looking for it to stitch you up.

I think I am better at surviving than I am at living. I thrive in the hazy afterglow of being crushed. Pick me up and toss me anywhere and I will find a way to still look up at the sky. I know how to pass the time so that I am someplace else. It's like I float up out of my body and I'm twelve again, hiding in the back of my closet or in the idea of being saved. The worst part is no was ever looking for me, so I'd fall asleep on the floor and hope that when I woke up there'd be a blanket draped across my shoulders. I've been grown up for a while now and I still haven't gotten the hang of chopping bell peppers or waiting for dough to rise. It amazes me that anyone has the patience to pickle beets or braid brioche. The currency I'm used to has always been silver and engraved with tomorrow. Haven't I lived long enough to know that the sand falls at the whim of my own hand? I've been saving it up, but for what, I still don't know.

for a moment,
I have
forgotten myself

DISASSOCIATE

I want to get out of my body
But I don't want to float into the clouds
Or disappear behind some trick mirror
Or sink into the couch
I want to to be cut open and I want
To grow flowers between my ribs
A garden without a fence
But today I am folded inside still
Balancing on the uneven hardwood
So I'll walk into the dim kitchen
Tear open a bag of Granny Smiths
Peel them over the sink and carve out the bruises
Toss them in cinnamon and sugar and
Mash cold butter into a bowl of oats and flour
For a moment, I have forgotten myself
But remembered my hands
Maybe that is all I am ever trying to do

DO I EXIST
IF YOU DO
NOT KNOW ME

GOLDFINCH

I told you I'm always afraid to die
Except when I'm reading Mary Oliver
I think one day a bird is going to fly into
My living room through the fireplace
And somehow I won't be afraid
Do forty-year-olds still fall in love like teenagers
Will I grow out of my hunger someday
Do you get to a point where there's nothing left
That feels new or stirring or worth staying up for
I don't know how anyone falls asleep at eight o'clock
Without feeling like they're missing something
I didn't used to understand disappearing
But now I think about picking up the turntable needle
Leaving a graveyard of past versions of myself behind
Will you forget me if I fade into the part of life
That isn't built upon parading through screens
Do I exist if you do not know me
It's so hard to stay awake to what's in front of me
I always find a way to slip out of my life

i hate being looked at
but i'd do anything
for you to see me

PHOSPHORESCENT

Have you ever held the sun in your hands
Sometimes I carry it around
In my pockets and forget it's there
Sometimes I feel so full of it that I believe in god again
What else is there besides
The streams of light peeking through magnolia leaves
Who am I to the baseball shirt
To the blazer or the black fishnets
Or the crooked bottom teeth
It doesn't matter
I smell lemon verbena laundry detergent
And it's like time travel
I'm in our West Hollywood apartment again
Falling asleep on my right hip
Sometimes I am forty-two but I am always fourteen
Do you see me on the page or in the sidewalk cracks
I wish I didn't care but I always do
Where does it come from
The longing
The need to be loved by the things that we love
I hear a song or read a poem and I'm on my knees
I hate being looked at but
I'd do anything for you to see me

DISAMBIGUATION

We are the only ones
Expected to find meaning
In our existence
No one cares what the
Squirrels do all day long

I want to live in
The woods so that
The bugs and
The rabbits can
Teach me
How to lie in the dirt

It is a comfort to know
That all I have to do is nothing
In the moments I am afraid
Of invisible things

Not much else in life is like that

OBLIVION

Someday I'll be too busy to notice the vampires
The sun wakes me up and I know who I am
Maybe the chaos will always be there but
I'll find a way to break it down into mulch and grow
Pears and herbs and gardenias from what's left of me
It takes a while to accept that the shadows matter
And I can't pretend to know the watermelon lollipop
Without the tongue that exists only to melt it away
To turn it into nothing until all that's left is a paper stick
It might feel like freedom now but it can't forever
I'll pull down the curtains and never snooze an alarm again
The worst thing I can think of is writing the same poem
Every day for the rest of my life and everyone knowing it
But me

i'm here now

but tomorrow

you might just

miss me

SOMEONE WHO DOESN'T EXIST

If the idea is better than the real thing, then I want to give you some dirt to work with. I want to tell you it was us in that apocalypse but instead I wash the dishes. I am grateful that you don't ask questions that will dissolve the illusion. We will always try to find a way to make peace with our own willful oblivion. Picture me, bent knees on the front steps as you walk by. I'm hoping you'll notice but I never look up until all I can make out is the ebb of knowing. The ageless lust of an elusive closeness. I waited till everything turned dark blue. Maybe I waited too long. I'm here now but tomorrow you might just miss me.

and beneath
each unturned morning
is a version of myself
i have yet to meet

WHO I REALLY AM

Maybe it isn't some hidden secret
Buried somewhere in the backyard
Or a fogged-up mirror poised for
A palm to wipe away the mist
Maybe it is something I am
Building every day with new hands
A story being written rather than
A mystery waiting to be solved
And beneath each unturned morning
Is a version of myself I have yet to meet
Who is eager to carry me through
Whatever it is that comes next

i'm afraid
i'll be gone
someday
never knowing
who i was
apart from
someone else's
story

FRANK O'HARA

Sometimes I feel like Frank O'Hara
Who never knew his real birthday
Spent his whole life thinking he was a Cancer
Turns out he was three months late
Born at the end of March like me
Late winter, early spring
Depends on how you look at things

I'm afraid I'll be gone someday
Never knowing who I was
Apart from someone else's story
I hate the thought of people getting buried
With secrets still hidden in their shame
Yet, here I am, undressing in front of you
Pretending that my nakedness is honesty

LINGER

I don't want to give you any more of me because
I'm not sure I'll get it back but
I don't want to be left alone
I feel the longing coming apart like ice thinning
On a backyard pond in the afternoon sun
I'm searching for the thirty-first day of November
I'm doing my best to draw out the end

YOU KNOW

I guess being busy is better than being left alone to spiral into the abyss of maladaptive delusion but sometimes I imagine what it would be like to hit pause. To read all day and to never do the dishes again. There is an empty beach somewhere and I can't help but feel like it misses me. A thick field of trees where the dirt smells like a parent. Yesterday, I was time traveling. I was eight, wearing a plaid jumper and Catholic school felt safe. The kind of safe where you don't even consciously understand you feel safe, you just do because the hallways are small and smell familiar, and your mother is waiting for you in the parking lot, and the boy across the street whose birthday is a few days before yours would lay down in the neighbor's backyard with you and stare at the sky until it got dark and you had to go home for dinner. It scares me to know that I will never feel that safe again because the greatest sense of safety is found in unknowing, and I know too much now. But I imagine what it would be like now to sit side by side in silence. To never have to speak another word because you already know anything I could say.

GRATEFUL

Music and poetry and the wind
and me, here—
awake for it all

I.

SUPERNOVA

It has been quiet like a freight train
passing through the night. Like a
hailstorm falling sideways. I can feel
the walls shaking from the railway cars
passing through the freezing rain. It's
almost midnight and I am an exploding
star glaring manically into the darkness.
Burning brightly and wildly like
I should have all these years. I am on
the edge of something. Fading into
Nothing. Waiting to become
Someone else.

TO FEEL SO
DIFFERENT
SO DISTANT
YET ENTIRELY
THE SAME

CHANGING SEASONS

I am waiting for my coffee
I am the old couple eating pastries
With their chairs turned toward the window
I am the wafting scent of musk and amber
I am the bright magenta trees lining route 240
Blooming in April while it rains
I am the veiny hands I know nothing about
Except that I wish they would touch me
I am gulping down the foam
Tasting the bittersweet memories on my tongue
The ones that have yet to happen
I am remembering what it means to have teeth
To feel so different, so distant
Yet entirely the same

PROOF

I like myself the most when I am alone

I am terrified of being alone

I like myself the most when I am terrified

OPEN

The daydreams aren't just daydreams anymore
I can get on the train whenever I'd like
The doors are wide open and waiting
For me to lie naked in the shifting light
Of a four-story Brooklyn walk-up
To fall asleep on a freckled chest
To run my fingers through fields of white sage
I am the opening iris
The floating dust that glimmers like crushed diamonds
The feathery eyelashes caught on eager fingers
I am the sunlight and the wind
Intersecting across the gleaming reservoir
Where the bluegills breathe underwater
Where you and I dance gloriously on the surface
Where we become carelessly entangled
Before slipping underneath

SOMETHING, TOGETHER

Dark and feathery and chirping, perched behind rigid organs, is a fluttering thing that whistles about the city and the blurry film photographs we'd take of us kissing and laughing dizzily in the shadows, where we can smile and fall in love with the glowing neon signs kept secret by passing strangers who do not know us but might be sad if they did. We are not sad at all. Not right now, anyway. We are teeming with the deep-down voices that never take the stage. Our hands squeeze each other's tightly until they don't. Until we say goodnight on some unpoetic corner that I'll memorize for the days when I am too old to be careless, tucking ourselves into different stories where we are both the hero and no one is the villain.

YOUR WILDFLOWER

Tighten your tanned arm around my waist
Put your thumb inside my bottom lip
Tell me how pretty I look in a dress
Even more with it on the floor
And with a sun-dripping smile
I will bloom beneath the ripened lust
That seeps from your secret gaze
Like a blazing hillside of orange poppies
Shifting toward you in the soft wind
Waiting to be crushed

please whisper
to the late
winter wind
that you still
think of me

SOMEONE YOU CAN'T FORGET

I attempt to escape to
A place where I have not lost
My allure, my softness
Please tell me. Wait. No, don't
Please whisper to the late winter
Wind that you still think of me

I must exist someplace
Where I glow boundlessly, still
Where I am an unanswered question
A what-if. A daydream
Retained unblemished in
Someone's memory

It's almost dark inside
My room and I am listening
To old songs in secret
My hands are cracked and
Bleeding from the cold

They do not see me
The way that you do

I tried holding myself
very still for a while

HONEST

The truth is,
I cannot be contained.
I cannot be taught to like water
More than orange juice.
I cannot pretend
For decades upon decades
(Years like soft footprints
And malnourished buzzards circling
Who I really am;
The whimsical part of me
Decaying like neglected cavities)
That I enjoy self-discipline
And going to the gym.
I cannot cook healthy dinners
And go to sleep at reasonable hours.
Not right now, anyway.
I will not wake up one morning
And be everything that you hoped I would be.
I tried holding myself very still for a while.
I tried to like doing what I'm supposed to.
And maybe I will someday,
But not because you told me to.

SWEETHEARTS

When I am at the reservoir watching strangers
Lower their metal boats into the water
I understand why people go to bars in search of stories
I blow my nose in old tissues while
A drug store filled with plastic wrapped Kleenex
Sits barely three miles down the road
I take it personally when small town boys
Settle for their hometown loves
They dig up their mix CDs from their old rooms
And think it is poetic
But there is nothing poetic apart from
Picking off all of my periwinkle nail polish
The yellow pine needles falling
In the valley of my open book
The cerulean blue T-shirt twisting silently
In a coffee shop window
Am I allowed to mourn the isolation
When I'm the one who dug the ditch
Perhaps the simplest of loves are the ones
Shared on Appalachian back roads
From the kind of boy that made
My twelve-year-old heart flutter
The family dinners at long wooden tables
And the kind of laughter that makes you
Forget what loneliness is
Maybe that's all I've really ever wanted
Maybe that's all I'll ever really need
The sound of gravel crunching
Under slow pickup truck tires and
Someone like you

ALIEN

I want to write about you
But I think it might be too soon

I am stopped on the cracked cement
Next to a small but needed park
In the middle of it all

There are hundreds of thousands of windows
Shut tightly to keep the cool air in

The only chickens for miles are being served up on plates
Between college roommates and lovers who find the city
More romantic than any vague resemblance of a kiss
Exchanged quickly on a narrow step

But still, I carry around my wicker basket
Packed with old egg cartons
And carefully folded tea towels

I memorize the feeling of tired eyes
That won't look away
Of how warm it is inside my bedroom
Tracing your outline in the dark

Until the soft orange light of morning
Paints every shadowy corner

Until I have found myself feral

Deep in the dark blue moonlight
Somewhere between you and the trees

I'M A NO ONE

I shouldn't know that you exist
But I wonder what surfaces we have both touched
Maybe a yellow crosswalk button in Santa Monica
Or a pair of sunglasses at Chelsea Market
I've never worried about sharing too much too quickly
It is something I do tirelessly and with praise
I attempted to trap you like fruit flies in vinegar
With flattery and eagerness and bare skin
But this time I wish I had drawn out the anticipation
Just a little bit longer
Wish I had given you the space to fidget in my silence
Maybe take out your notebook and jot something down
About the sky and how I'm not blonde but close enough
Instead you write poems about your ex
And I laugh at myself for believing that perhaps
I could have meant something to you

A STRANGER TO REALITY

Illusions aren't shattered
They excuse themselves quietly
Into a crowd of faceless indifference
They turn the corner and disappear into
Bright alleyways where
No footprints are left to follow
Where you do not wish to find them
Where it is forgotten that you ever
Held onto the hand of a hope
That does not exist

TALKING TO THE CEILING

I am not afraid of all the ways
That you could hurt me

Your words bounce off me
Like hail the size of golf balls
The width of years spent wondering
Why I still think of you
The weight of never
Grasping your impermanence
The sound of ice shattering and
Echoing unanswerable questions like
Will you ever be okay
And will I ever really know

I will not make the same mistakes
I will not keep hurting you
For the sake of nostalgia
And my own unfinished feelings

None of it makes sense yet
I hold it in my heart
With all the hysterical remembering
Of an underexposed photograph
It will live there forever or
More realistically speaking
Until it breaks down in the dirt
With everything else that I am

You crash into me like fog
Filling the space between tinted windows
Drifting through unlit streets

I imagine it is the same for you
The remembering and the forgetting

The inability to give without taking

The unrelenting nature of longing
For something that is not yours

I would like for
it to be me

EARNEST

I am nothing if not aspirational
Sometimes naively
Sometimes to the point of embarrassment
But I'll never be embarrassed, not really
Not of being hopeful, not of not caring
If my wants are too far-off or unlikely or vulnerable
I will still frolic, still slip my blouse off pale shoulders
Pull my knotted hair away from the nape of my neck
Inviting you to sink your teeth into me

The daisies in virgin fields are waiting, unpicked
To be threaded together into something
To be worn by anyone at all
If not me, then someone else

I would like for it to be me

HEALING

I am constantly wanting to
Lie down on the earth
When the anxious energy
Inside me feels far too heavy
But I am afraid of all
The things that could sting me
The little bugs that might
Crawl into the tiny cuts that
Mysteriously appear on
My knuckles and shins
If only the grass was
Mowed and combed through
If only someone were to
Lay out a soft quilt in the shade
Just for me

STILL YOURS

I was riding in the passenger seat
Down a meandering stretch of back road
Where the mountains look like watercolors
When I realized that your arms feel safer
Than my own mother's

(I am afraid of what that means)

I still fall asleep in the old grey t-shirt that
Your dad brought home from Scotland
Still think of you every time
I pull a sundress over my head

(I am afraid of what that means)

The braids in my hair
The buzzing in my chest
The left side of the bed
The small, persistent voice inside
Telling me to keep going

Are all somehow
In some way
Still yours

And I am somehow
In too many ways
Still yours

SIMPLER

Two hares are
Chasing one another
In the tall grass
The wind smells like
The past
Like soccer practice
Like Sugar Hollow
Summer camp
Where we didn't
Shower for a week
Could it really
Be as simple
As falling asleep
In an open
Field under
Flickering stars and
Flashing satellites
Feeling the
Earth closely
Beneath
Waking up
Damp from
The morning dew

SITTING IN THE DRIVEWAY

If I sit outside for the
Rest of my life
Perhaps nothing can
Hurt me

I always feel safe
Among the white flower weeds
The cricket songs and
The birds chattering
Remind me I am only all
That they are
And if they are always there
Then I guess I am too

THE REAPER

If I fear
The world is
Conspiring to kill me
Or distrust my
Ability to take care
Of myself
To the point of
Avoidance and freezing
And unliving
Then I am
Already dead

LIFE IS TOO SHORT TO NOT LOVE YOU

I am scrounging my room for things that smell like you
I wish you wore cologne because I would have braved my
Fear of shopping malls just to be able to hold on to you
A little longer

I would have doused myself with the memory of you

II.

The leaves will be
turning orange soon.
I almost forgot.

I WANT TO TAKE CARE OF MYSELF

This time next week, I will be breathing the air that I've been gasping for. I didn't realize that four months could feel like four broken bones. Two arms, two legs, all secretly cracked, only felt under the weight of my own invisible dread. It's okay that I went back to being sixteen for awhile. It's not what I wanted, what I planned, but it's what happened.

I woke up with butterflies in my stomach and the rug ripped out from under me. My car sits in the driveway and I don't drink coffee anymore because it makes me shake and I don't know how to handle the shaking like I used to. I never used to worry about sharing drinks yet today I've washed my hands fifteen times and still don't trust them. But it's August and I'm twenty-three again. Or at least I will be when the key slides into the lock and I take that big gulp and pray for it to add a few years back that were taken this summer.

Everything is a circle cut in half, alternating between hollow and whole, snaking through time with hysterical pseudo endings and beginnings that are really just doors leading down a different hallway in the same goddamn infinite hotel. Sometimes Wes Anderson's, sometimes The Shining. I don't have to listen to the screaming for the rest of my life if I don't want to. I don't have to be so unhappy if I don't want to. Maybe next Saturday I will drive to the coffee shop on the corner and order something decaf and sugary and thank god that it's over. It's over. Holy shit.

The leaves will be turning orange soon. I almost forgot.

I WANT TO LET YOU BACK IN

I have always been the type to run
Toward a fire dripping with oil
It wasn't until recently that I began
Collecting vats of concrete to pour
Around my heart; believing love is
Not mine to keep
At least the kind that is doughy like
The chunky arms of a toddler
Or mango mochi ice cream softening
On the kitchen counter

When you began to comb through me
Like virgin sand with a slow and gentle
Attentiveness I'd never seen before
It felt like pin pricks all the way down
The length of my spine
The hair on my arms stood straight up
Like cattails swaying hypnotically in the
Marsh that lies outside of time
Beside the long unbending road to the
Beach that has not changed since the
Summer you were small and dipped
New toes into the sea

I thought the dissonance I felt in my chest
When you looked at me was some deep
Down greater voice telling me that there
Was such a thing as right and wrong—
A voice that I was not wise
Enough to discern but should accept—
It told me to be seen like this

Or by you or right now was somehow
Something I should run away from
With braids whipping behind me in the
Thick warm wind until I reached a
Secluded spot in the shade where
I could hide and scream and not have
To think about tomorrow

But then the spaces between our
Entanglement grew wider and
I thought you must have found a way
To shimmy out of the longing
And I felt cold   stuck   afraid in my
Seclusion—like I had misplaced a
Four-leaf clover just as the sun had
Dried up all the green things left on
Earth; all the trees now bare in the
Forest I sought to camouflage myself
From the light that was dying to reach me

And then I realized that the walls I'd built
Were not keeping me from harm

But instead had allowed me to harm myself
Without interruption

THE HAPPY YEARS

At night I dream of sun-drenched eggshell walls
Baking in the morning like Yukon Gold potatoes
Where we wake unbothered by the encroaching light
I'll meet you in the kitchen to switch on the toaster
The coffee pot, pulling our ceramic mugs
From the drying rack
Carrying our books with bent covers to the balcony
Where you set down thick slices
Of French bread slathered in butter
A bowl of fresh cold strawberries
On a small round table that we found
At a Sunday yard sale two summers ago

We take turns taking crisp bites
In between sips of steaming coffee
Mine with raw honey and cream, yours black
Our oily thumbs staining the corners
Of thin ivory pages
I listen to the sound of you reading;
Of the world waking up
Birds singing their sunrise songs—
And my heart
Slow, and buoyant, and irrevocably yours

THE SOUND OF SIRENS AS I FALL ASLEEP

I cannot live in isolation with my anxiety. I never want to live in the suburbs or outskirts of a town again, at least not until I've become much stronger, much less likely to regress. I need to be in the middle of it all or else I will be left alone to fall apart. You'd assume I would benefit from the peace and quiet and lack of traffic and one-lane roads. But they make me small. I need to walk to a coffee shop on the days when I can barely get out of bed. I need to drive for a few minutes and pass by dozens of restaurants and stores and places with people. Places I can make it to on my bad days. Where I can grab some tea and remind myself that the world isn't as dreadful as my brain likes to pretend it is. Otherwise, I will get stuck inside and I'll forget what it's like to love listening to music in my car and to love the sun and the city and the people. I have to step outside and quickly be reminded of the beauty and the possibility and the good stuff. To snap myself out of the spiraling defeated internal monologue that's meekly accepting that maybe I'll never drive again, travel again, feel independent and sufficient again. It's all bullshit but so easy to believe when I'm stuck. When the trees are closing in and I can't wash away the feeling of detachment. So I need to plant myself in places where it's much harder to become stiff. I have to be in the middle. I will wither if I'm not. I won't do that to myself again.

LITTLE SPARROW

Will I be able to live my entire life afraid of microwaves
I turn on every light in the house to feel safe
The little table lamp by the stairs
The secondhand string lights, the bathroom light
All of them
It is two in the afternoon. I do not believe in ghosts
I eat spoonfuls of hummus and stale pita chips
With only my right hand because
I used my left to open the cupboard
I should be taking a vitamin D supplement but
The gummies remind me of dead things and
The chewable tablets taste like old gauze
I'm worried my poetry is beginning to sound like
Too specific digressions
What is the theme? The big picture? The point of it all
Sometimes it feels like I am still a child
A yellow chick fluttering around in the grass
Mouth wide open, waiting for the sky to fall into me

TAKE ME

Something about you, something about October
The dried up leaves and the way
Everything feels quiet in the middle of the day
Like living inside of a VHS tape that
Hasn't been rewound in a decade or two
Makes me want to start visiting the cemetery
Make friends with the forgotten
When we ended up walking the dogs there on accident
It felt like coming home
I'll bring my books and a bag of dried cherries
Peanut butter, bars of dark chocolate wrapped in gold foil
Sunflower seeds, the nightstand with the warped wooden
Drawer that's always getting stuck
Where I keep the half-melted birthday candles
And a box of matches, just in case
Prop my pillow up against a headstone
Read Vonnegut until I fall asleep
Grow closer to death until it doesn't scare me anymore
I used to think ghosts lived in mausoleums
But now I know
They live inside of twenty-four-year-olds
Who watch the same vampire movie every time it rains
Just to feel safe inside the familiarity of the past
I'm still the eighteen-year-old girl
Just waiting for something to happen to her
I burn my skin in the shower to feel less alone

when I bore the weight
of feeling everything
I mistook the trembling
for weakness
when all along
it was the pulse of strength

A RENAISSANCE

How heartbreaking is it
That I've been holding myself up with
The same shaky knees
That did not buckle
When I was certain they would
The ones I nick in the shower
From time to time
And apologize silently
To blameless skin
While blood rinses down my shins

When I bore the weight
Of feeling everything
I mistook the trembling
For weakness
When all along
It was the pulse of strength
All my nerve endings
Crying out like newborns
The watermark of being alive

I just want you to see me

CHANGE ME

When I'm alone
I dance in spaces
Void of you
And I am afraid
Of the brazen voice
Inside my chest
That twirls
The daydream of
Solitude
Around her fingers
I am afraid the truth
Is buried deep
Inside of me
Folded tightly with
Hospital corners
Suffocating my
Ability to say what I mean
And I suppose I just
Want you to see me but
Too often it feels
As though you are
Gazing into
A mud-clouded puddle
Of yesterday's rainwater
Seeing only a vague
Reflection of
Yourself and
Of who you wish
I could be

i think about
seeping into the
ambient noise
of someone else's life
all the time

YOUR AFFECTION

I cannot keep orchids alive
And I lose all my gold rings
I don't know how to be a pretty thing
But I know how to shrink
My life down into a few square miles
Into an even smaller screen
Reflecting shadows and empty stomachs
Grasping for Minute Maid
And strawberry toaster pastries
Is it enough to exist
Somewhere in the middle
Are love songs written in Kansas City
I think about seeping into the ambient noise
Of someone else's life all the time
One day I will walk into the bookshop
Or maybe into one of your dreams
Appearing exactly as I am
Saltwater and blurry around the edges
Plain like North Dakota terrain
And cracked open on the surface of truth
Your heart, like scratched vinyl
Or late February, will skip
When you look at me

WHERE OUR LOVE LIVES

Between the static
laughter of telephone lines
and the sun, rising

FOR MY MOTHER

Often, I forget that my eyes look just like yours
That they have seen me as I've waded through each phase
Many of which have held pain that we both share

I forget that when I think about how I wish
That you brushed my hair more when I was a little girl
That I don't know if anyone ever brushed yours
Or whether hands remind you of something
Soft to hold or tight fists closed to warmth

When I think of your spine, I imagine it curved
Like a waning crescent from all the years of feeling small
Under the weight of the world, unable to stand tall
And face it all with your chest open to the sky

But I hope that when you hold yourself at night
You rub your fingers over the skin of your elbows
Which have always healed just as you have
Always risen from the deep dark that follows you around

I think when they voted you best legs in high school
It was a promise, a premonition that you would always
Somehow find a way to carry yourself through
Everything that was coming
That you would never stop walking forward
Into the next storm, looking toward the sun

Waiting for the clouds to break

RUSHIE

I feel like my grandfather in the morning
Drinking instant coffee and eating white toast with butter
I was too young to know him well but I do
Know that he loved bingo and drew funny cartoons
And collected dogs and antiques and that
He spent his whole life hiding part of himself
And sometimes it keeps me up at night
Thinking about the world he could have known
Had he felt the freedom to or maybe if
He hadn't smoked so many cigarettes
I like to think that if he were still around
We would sit across from one another
In the kitchen on Washington Street
Eating banana twin pops next to that big arched window
Spending afternoons laughing or in comfortable silence
Until the sun rose low enough to beam across
The black and white checkered vinyl flooring
I would tell him that his secrets are safe with me

OLD FRIEND

I want to call you and tell you that
My dog doesn't bark at the sound of the stove lighting
Or the ding of the toaster oven anymore
And that I moved the arm chairs out
From in front of the window
And the room is brighter now
And I wonder if that would've made you feel
More at home
And maybe you would have stayed

SCANNING THE SKY

My birthday is in less than a week
And I'm regretting every horror movie I've watched
Because they give me scenes to play back
In my head when I close my eyes

I wish I didn't know what walnuts tasted like
Wish I didn't know what to look for
When my room gets dark from the rain outside

I know now that it was out of love
When my friend's mom created the rule of
No webcams behind closed doors

Maybe a little suffocation would've felt
Better than the cherry pit in my stomach
As a fourteen-year-old girl lifting up my shirt
For a man I met in a chat room
When he told me I didn't have to be so shy

COFFEE BREATH

You started drinking coffee after I left
And now I smile into your mouth
When I taste it on your breath

It often feels
as though
I exist only
in winter
or summer —
never both

TREMBLING ASPEN

I am grateful to the birds who wake each morning
And sing of hope on slender branches
In the raw and early months as well as all the others
A tireless reminder of what is always there
They are not aware nor do they care
About the state of my heart
Whether it is light or numb or beating at all

It often feels as though I exist
Only in winter or summer—never both

I am indebted to the body
Lying next to me at dawn
And all the ways that it remembers
The things I so easily forget

i keep my hunger to myself

MOTHERING MYSELF

I wish my mom lived ten minutes away
I'd drive to her house
Just to spend the day sitting in silence
Next to something breathing

I dream about the comfort of a safety net
In crowded cafes where no one gives
A damn about my fear of dying
Before I am ready
And yet I'm sure if I asked for a hand
I would be answered with warmth

But I do not ask
I skip breakfast and drink iced lattes
I keep my hunger to myself
I find more ways to quiet the growl

There is a patch of sun
waiting for me to step into it
just beyond the shadows

TANDEM

Life is painful but
It is also whistling sparrows
And six o'clock light in the spring
And falling asleep with my dog
Curled up right below my chin
And getting lost in really good writing
And putting on a sundress
That has been hanging in my closet for a year

It is the velvet stretches of nothing
In between unbearable aching
That make it feel like maybe
There is a patch of sun
Waiting for me to step into it
Just beyond the shadows

even now, i feel myself
drifting from the page,
unable to keep myself woven
tightly through what i love

ALL OF ME

The things I love the most I do not spend enough time emerged in. I don't know why. Maybe because it is easier to engage in experiences that cannot be measured. Maybe because if I sit down to write and nothing comes out I will feel the poet I've known slip from my fingers. Or if I spend the afternoon reading but the kitchen sink is still full of dishes it will not feel deserved. Because there is always something more to be doing. I like to think that I would spend my perfect day somewhere underneath a big oak tree, reading and writing and laughing with you. Picking through the grass for four-leaf clovers as the dogs chase their tails and unintentionally kick up tufts full of them. Even now, I feel myself drifting from the page, unable to keep myself woven tightly through what I love.

SUNBATH

I think what I am looking forward to the most is never being without a window. In every room there will be light. I can pull up my hair and lean into the mirror, patting serums into flushed cheeks with diffused light inviting itself in through the frosted bathroom glass. I can make coffee and sit on the porch and try as hard as I can to root myself in the morning rather than waiting around for the moon. I can open the glass door of my study and read books in an overstuffed arm chair without needing a lamp; and I will write, if I am heavy enough, if I am open enough. I can stretch out on the couch in the living room padded by the warm bodies of my dogs on either side. I can be blissful or spent or numb, and the sun will still chassé down the walls. I can sit at the dining room table, eating jasmine rice and chana masala, and the floor will be painted in an orange goodbye. One day, I will be sitting in a garden with a book, my head thrown back laughing, and none of this will touch me anymore.

III.

I seem to miss
the things I made
sure would never
happen to me

ANNA KARENINA

It doesn't have to mean anything more
Than a crumpled up dollar bill in an open guitar case
I hope one day I'll learn to keep my head down
To keep walking instead of getting stuck
In front of windows
It feels like I'm loitering in the parking lot
Of everyone else's lives
A heap of squeezed ginger ale cans
And candy bar wrappers crowding my bare feet
I guess eventually I'll have to leave and find out
Things always look better through a side mirror
I glance back and see the orange trees in the median
A runner almost getting hit by a left turn
I'm so glad I didn't have to watch her die
Instead I watch two college students nervously laugh
Shifting their weight from one foot to the other
Beside the crosswalk button and I sigh a little
They are on one side of the glass and I am on the other
I seem to miss the things I made sure
Would never happen to me
Tuck myself into bed buzzing with the engine of
A snow-covered train, a reckless ellipses
It is comforting to want what I cannot have

I HOPE
THE TRUTH
SPLITS YOU
IN TWO

SUCH A SWEET GIRL

Kindness is not a closed mouth
Smile and a closed fist
A flower with thorns thrown at tired feet
Watch as the petals are plucked off
And the stems are shoved back
Into a palm until it bleeds
I hope the truth splits you in two
Like an axe to a log
I hope you feel the sun as it lights up
All of your ugly and cobwebbed corners
I hope you hear the way kindness
Roars like a summer storm
I hope it makes you want
To dig up the earth with your bare hands
Dirt beneath your fingernails
To never see a rosebush the same

i want more of you
to wrap around me
at night

COLLIDE

I want more of you to wrap around me at night when the heat is off but there's still enough sweat to stick my thighs to the top sheet. I want to circle my own prayers and find ways to say them better. I want to get tired of the obvious and write more about the creaking car door or the busted lip. Take me out into the vacant lot, the Sunday service, the falling asleep with the TV on. I'll get used to the backyard fire pit, the smoke following me around. I like the way it clings to my clothes until I run them through the wash. I'll make a copy of your house key and let myself in when I can't get the words right. I saw the grocery list on the refrigerator door. I already have it memorized.

maybe almost failing
feels a little bit like
cheating death

IF A YELLOW TRAFFIC LIGHT WAS A GIRL

Maybe I leave it all till the last minute
because some gritty part of me enjoys
the rapid pulse of pulling back right
before the truck turns the corner and
blows through the stretch of hot
asphalt I was just lying down and
burning my skin on. It tears down the
road, out of sight, and I've still got all
my limbs intact. Maybe almost failing
feels a little bit like cheating death, like how
breathing feels after a contest of who
can hold it longer in the motel pool,
or how good a glass of ice water
tastes after downing a bag of potato
chips. There are plenty of hours in the
day. I could wake up before the sun
rises or sleep in till noon and it
wouldn't make much of a difference.
I'm just a girl who loves the taste of
barely scraping by.

WHOLESOME

I want to be like peanut butter banana bread
Like a red brick house with a low front porch
Where the dog and the old cat and
The greying sweethearts sit in chenille silence
While dusk settles in and the grasshoppers
Out-sing the downtown traffic
You know, they've got real candles flickering
In the black lanterns by the french doors
I wonder if we'll ever own a trophy like that
Blissful in our rocking chairs and nothing left to say
Except I love you, every once in a while
When the neighbors remind us
Just how lucky we are

ORDINARY TENDERNESS

1. We put up shelves in the kitchen
so we could clear off the countertops
and cook without all the clutter

2. You told me to listen to piano music
and turn off my phone and you were right

3. The salt and vinegar chips you picked up
while you were at the grocery store

4. Some 1970s handwritten casserole recipe
with black eyed peas and cottage cheese
you baked that I thought I would hate but
it was exactly the comfort meal I needed

5. When you fed me Tylenol out of your palm
because my head hurt too badly to move

6. And then we fell asleep on opposite
ends of the couch and I knew this was the
kind of love I'd hoped I would end up with
when I was seventeen and daydreaming
about what my life would look like someday

maybe I won't be broken forever

SIDELINES

I spend my days clinging to the idea
That the roads are made of wet pine needles
And if I lay down on the edge of trying
I'll be swallowed up by a flock of crows
Isn't it funny how I tire myself in the pursuit of
Calloused hands and warm shoulders and snails
But I like it best when I'm driving with an
Empty passenger seat and I take a loop around
The neighborhood just to hear the end of a song
I remember myself when I sit in the dark and
The night tastes like saltwater, like honey
I won't get much sleep tonight but
Maybe I'll make pancakes on Saturday
Maybe I won't be broken forever

HOW TO BE SMALL

Every night I fold myself up
Like a wrinkled fitted sheet
I don't pay any attention to
The edges I just wrap it
Around my clenched fist
So it takes up less space
My therapist once pointed
Out that I hold my breath
And get really still without
Realizing it but now I notice
It all the time and I wonder
When it began but not really
Because I know that I was
Taught to soak the heels of
Others and work out their
Splinters before my own
It sounds kind but it's not
How do you see an empty
Space and decide that it
Is yours to run through
Can you teach me to look up
At the mountains and then
Down at my own feet

RELENTLESS

There is a car alarm going off
In the neighborhood and
I've turned up the radio as
Loud as it will go
I've stuffed my ears with foam
I shut all the windows and
I shoved towels in the gaps
Below the doors
Now I'm nailing egg cartons
To the wall
The rhythm seems to pace
With my heart
I have forgotten what it was like
Before the noise
I have done everything but
Pick up my keys

FIVE MORE MINUTES

I've lost it. I'm not sure what it is, but it's gone
When you lift the veil and break the fourth wall
My stomach feels like swallowtails and
The sirens sound like laughter and one day
They'll be coming for me and I won't be ready
How long have I known this and
How long have I not changed a thing
It costs less to fade into the noise
But it pays more to scream along with it
Which I guess is why I'm here
And why I'm sometimes not
I tell myself that at least we're descending together
And hold out for the gut-punch that returns
My breath instead of taking it away
We stand side by side digging our graves
Passing notes back and forth
Hoping that they might mean something

777

You don't think you'll ever forget to put the lid
Back on the blender before you turn it on
And then you do
I hate the wind because it does what it wants
And I don't know if I want to control it or be it
You went to the store without me to pick up eggs
Loaves of bread to put in the freezer, paper towels
Pomegranates and green bananas
I should've gone with you but I have this feeling
In my chest that I'm worried won't go away
Until I climb back into bed and start over
In the morning
I've been trying to wake up all day
The sun is down now and I feel like a girl
Who doesn't know how to walk away from the
Blue light of a slot machine
I'm sitting on the floor in front of the mirror
Braiding my hair the way you like and waiting
For you to come home and forgive me
Like you always do and like I never deserve

POCKET CHANGE

Everything is the last bite of chocolate bourbon pie
My laptop screen is cracked and a part of me knows
That I like when things get broken because then
The pressure of maintaining wholeness dissolves
I like getting up early and I like staying up late
When the hours feel like stealing caramels
From the crystal jar on the table by the front door
Funny how I forget that I can turn on the radio
Open a window and lie down the floor if I need to
I wanted something sweet and then I remembered

TWO FRUIT FLIES

Two fruit flies
chasing each other
around the edge
of a glass ramekin
full of orange marmalade
reminded me
of us

STUMBLE

I left the light on because I was afraid
and it was easier to fall asleep pretending
that I could fake daylight forever, but
then the bulb burned out and now I can't
see my hand in front of my face. I don't
want to spend another twenty dollars on
a pack of 60 watts. I rather let my eyes
adjust to the pitch black and stumble
toward the doorway until I find the latch
and put enough space between my body
and the bed that I have made for it.

HELD

There's a moss covered lake dug up between what I share with you and what sits on the back of my tongue. At night, I stand in front of the bathroom mirror and try to scrape it off with a toothbrush, but the green film algae feeds off of angst. I suck my teeth and taste the underside of pontoon boats and warm beer. I'm scared of drowning but I wait with my legs hanging over the edge of the dock, wishing someone would push me in just to get the thrashing over with. I fantasize about sinking deep into the candor. When I feel the seaweed brush up against my ankles and my feet find the bottom, I'll dig my toes into the sand. The 104-acre reservoir will dry up around me and I'll be standing there in a crater in some desert where my spit tastes like agave and there is nothing left unsaid.

MATCHSTICK

What use is this wall socket if I am
Too afraid to stick a bobby pin in it
If I don't fill myself up with its veracity
Let it flow through me like a revelation
I used to be such a good conduit for
The regularly buried sensations and so
Eager to lift up my shirt and show you what
I spend all day hiding from everyone else
But now I find myself tensing up at my
Own thoughts before sending them away
I think I'm better when I strike myself
Against the hard truths and gut feelings
Pressed up against my uncertainties
Lit to compensate for a pushy darkness
Maybe not better for the woodpile or
The pyrophobic or the prude but for
Those of us who like to watch things burn

BLINK

I hit the curb and
Heard the tire pop
I wish I'd pulled
The wheel sooner but
I didn't and
I don't keep a spare
In the trunk
Never got around to
Replacing the last
I'm on the side
Of the road
Waiting for a savior
Maybe I'm waiting
For myself
But I hate myself
For letting go
I thought the road
Could go on forever
If I willed it to
If I ignore the
Check engine light
Then nothing's
Really broken
If I close my eyes
Then maybe
Crashing will feel
Like flying

I'll wrap
myself
around you

OVEREXPOSED

Come here. I'll wrap myself around you
Most of the time I'm sure I'm a sliding glass door
Obvious like a schoolgirl crush
Never able to hide the pink in my cheeks
Or bury the truth behind enough broken parables
I'm about as vigilant as a Chihuahua
Perched on top of a sofa barking at the mailman
Forgetting for a moment that you could pick me up
And put me down on the floor but
I promise I'll just jump back up again
Never fully accepting the plainness of my bluff
The winters crack my knuckles but
I don't want to buy another pair of gloves
I've got ripped fingernails turned bloody
And a kitchen sink full of unwashed mugs
And you're pulling my hands away from my face
Trying to show me how much we look the same

IT FEELS GOOD
TO PRETEND

AESTHETIC

We're living in our faux leather worlds trying to pawn them off on anyone who's paying. The memories are real but the remembering is not. Or maybe it's the other way around. Wouldn't it be nice if it were true. Sometimes I slip into delusion like a silk dress with a price tag I can't afford. I promise myself I'm just trying it on but god it feels good to pretend. Even for a second. A sneeze behind the wheel. A finger on the fogged window. A spaced-out gaze you forget to break. When I take off the absence it feels heavier than before. What I wouldn't give to believe you.

SYMBIOTIC

Even in the deep grey I still find myself
Falling in love with the fistless fight
I think most of this has to do with you
And how every day you have kept me fed
The hunger never ends but neither do the plates
They just keep coming through the swing door
Piling up on the table till I'm ready to pick up a fork
Certainly there is always someone who gets it—
The persistent pursuit of grasping at fullness
Or at least, who can relate to a varying appetite
I may never know a windless day but
At least I have a kite and two cheese sandwiches
Wrapped in a paper towel, and you, with your
Extra set of hands and a growling stomach and
Nowhere else to be—at least until the sun sets
We can keep each other company

IV.

i'm still here

waiting

to be found

SELF PORTRAIT AS A SILVER HOOP

Are you looking for me
In the last place you remember
I'm a lost earring under
Some hotel pillow or
At the bottom of the pool
Trying to reflect the light
Trying to catch your eye
Where do I go when
You get tired of the hunt
When the bed gets made
And the vacation ends
And I'm still here
Waiting to be found

FOOTING

Step outside and feel
The cool air on your skin
Listen to the whir of cars
Or the crickets
The thump of your heart
Let it all fall around you like water
Like wax like a wildfire
Sink into the waves
And the warmth
Dig your toes into the grass
And know for certain
By the way the sun peeks
Through the glossy leaves
Of a magnolia tree
That hope is an exhale
It is a sparrow
It is you

HARD TIMES

The waiting becomes like pulling at the corners of a patchwork quilt until there are no wrinkles left. The truth is, there is no such thing as a marble blanket. There will always be the creases and the feelings that won't flatten, no matter how hard we tug at their edges. We were never meant to spend all day running our hands over fault lines. All we can really do is keep unmaking the bed.

it takes
all morning
to claw
myself out
of the dread

SWING BY

It takes all morning to claw myself out of the dread. Some days the instant coffee can't shake me awake enough to find a pulse so I press two fingers against a different neck and pretend it's mine. I know I'm getting careless with the drift. It's a bag of ice to a snake bite and a mouth full of blood. I only ever want to go to the store when it's closed. In a different life, I'm running down the aisles and you're barely keeping up. Will you sit with me while I swallow the ghosts? I'm tired of staring at an unopened blister pack.

RITUAL

It takes guts made of silk to keep spinning these webs each time they are broken, still eager to catch anything worth wrapping myself around. I don't think I'll ever stop weaving hunger through patches of sky while the sun sinks further into tomorrow, tucking paper napkins into my collar, seeing slices of strawberry rhubarb pie between the clouds. I set my trap between two unlikely branches at dusk and eagerly wait for beautiful, buzzing things to stray from their flight paths and crash into me.

AGORAPHOBIA

What does it feel like
To want something so badly
That you're willing to pull away
From the curb with your
Playlist and your fear
I can't imagine myself alone for
Four hours on the highway
I can't imagine believing
That I belong in the world
I close my eyes and picture
Getting home by dinner time
Trunk full of boxes
Ready to build a life that
I've so forcefully taken
Maybe she existed once before
Maybe someday I will meet her again

TALKING TO MYSELF

My boyfriend is mixing concrete in the backyard
And I can't remember your name

I spend so much time remembering
It often feels like I'm the only one

Trudging through the void
Of moments that have died

Trying to flip over corpses so I can
Press my ear to their chest and hear my name

Even though I know they are gone and
I shouldn't be looking anyway

I hold onto moments much longer than I should
So often I choose the comfort of my inner world

The place I've retreated to ever since I was a little girl
Where I learned that I could endure my life

If I hid there while everything around me burned
Over what's right in front of me

FARAWAY

It seems like all I've ever wanted was for someone
to hold me and tell me it would be okay but no
one is ever able to. Not my parents, not you.
It'll always be just me, feeling like an idiot for
asking for anything as the door slams in my face,
wrapping my arms around myself as I always
have. Always will. What can I do to make someone
believe I deserve to be held. Why do I have to
be brave to be worthy of comfort. Why is making
it to twenty-four not brave enough. Why does it
feel like everyone sees me more clearly from a distance
than anyone who's standing up close

ALL I WANT
IS TO FEEL SEEN

DIZZY

When I look at you, I see myself surrounded by all of my circling doubts, the voices of others, maybe the voice of reason. But all I want is to believe you. All I want is to feel seen. Maybe because in many ways, I am still sixteen. I hope that I can become someone who exists in the present instead of sifting through the past because it's what is familiar. Someone who's okay with being forgotten. Who doesn't have to return the favor of remembering. But I know how good it feels to be thought of. I hope you're doing okay out there. You remind me of myself.

[redacted] LOSER [redacted]

[redacted] the first time [redacted]
a man [redacted] took a bite out of [redacted]
My flushed cheeks [redacted]
I thought [redacted]
I was [redacted] ready [redacted]
He [redacted] smiled, showing [redacted]
himself [redacted]
to [redacted]
a teenager with cut up thighs. [redacted]
I fantasize about [redacted]
his smirk fading into panic [redacted]
I wish the [redacted]
blood on his hands [redacted] was not mine. [redacted]

SECONDHAND

I hear you calling my name in the silence
I hear your voice in my head while
I wash the dishes

I want nothing left to protect
I want to be naked in the grass

I have become obsessed with rain and the moon
Broken-hearted at its shyness in the summer
I stand behind a glass door—I cannot close my eyes

The clouds tease a storm that never comes and
I keep waiting for something to touch me

NEEDY

I know it
Sounds stupid
But sometimes
I hold both
Of my hands
Together
And pretend
That one of
Them is yours

CAN YOU SEE ME

I do not like being in pain alone
When will I learn to rub my own back
Play with my own hair
I am in a soft bed
This is the only place I would like to be
And yet
I am writhing
Wondering how I will make it through the day
With no one around
To witness my suffering

i'll never stop trying
to give you my hand

NURTURE

How do I convince myself
That my limb is not my limb
Your fingers look like mine
And when I stick a pinky
Knuckle deep in the soil
And hook it inside my cheek
It tastes like I expect it to
I don't have to pull up
The roots to know that
They hold the same rot as mine
But I can't keep them
From growing further into
The damned rocks
Can't raise the beds at arm's length
Sweating glass on the edge of the bar
Shrinking subway car
Red light and an anvil foot
I'll be right here the whole time
I'll never stop trying to give
You my hand

IN YOUR BACK POCKET

I wait for you all day
I stare at myself in the mirror
Not to see what I look like
But to study how
You must see me
Posed in front of some tiny window
Like those plastic keychain souvenirs
I got my mom to buy from
A man who would run down
The Ocean City shoreline
Expensive camera on a strap
Around his neck
Offering to take our photograph
I imagine that's what it must be like
Squinting down at me
Some hundreds of miles away
Small and blurry and partly imagined
Carried around in your pocket
Silent alongside the keys
Rattling in your hand as you
Unlock the front door
And step into a life
Achingly distant from mine
You, kicking off your shoes
Setting your phone on
The nightstand
Turning out the light

ARE YOU SURE

Sore stomach and tears in my teeth
Rusted tin man with an empty chest
Holding a silk pouch full of
Sawdust and mourning the unlucky
Bugs in the woods while the rest carry on
Carelessly oblivious and happier for it
I don't like working too hard for it
Because the glass gets harder to look at
When I feel like I'm not ready for it and
I always want to be ready for it
I'm hiding inside an armor of
Wishful thinking only to be found
Out in the ultraviolet turning red
With my face in your hands and broken
Egg yolks dripping between our fingers
I'll lick them clean if the hospital
Will give me a room with a view

You know what you're getting
Yourself into, don't you

EASY KID

I'm no good under pressure
I've got enough weight to carry

I used to get yelled at for
Walking on my heels
So I learned to sneak around
On the balls of my feet

How to slowly turn the knob
Back into the lock so that
It wouldn't click when I closed it

Behind the door I figured out
How to be loud without making a sound

I liked the dusty vent, the outlet
The vacuum, the empty space
Better when it held me
Back before I tried to hold it
Back before I tried to draw a line around it

I would pick up my little sister
From her crib and bounce her
On my hip and pretend
That I was soothing her
When really I was soothing myself

Maybe some things are better off scattered
Where no one will attempt to wrap
A white picket fence around them

It gets too heavy when you try
To fit it all in a box and
Drag it across the yard

Wild blades that were
Never meant to be bought

i write down the things
i feel but cannot say

I'M A GOOD GIRL

I'm hanging in there. There being the narrow margins
where I write down the things I feel but cannot say

I can't shake the sorrow of wanting
not only to be seen but to be sought out

It seems like the best thing
I could ever be is easy

You were kidding when you said that
I'm not the center of anyone's universe

But I cried anyway
as soon as you left the room

It's desperate if you want it
and you only get it if you don't

I don't know how to not want it
and I only want it if I don't have to ask

There are too many questions with answers
I cannot bring myself to face

i learn how to
make myself smaller

I'M A SAD GIRL

I don't want to be sad but I am. It's not the sinking kind of sad. It's a heavy sad, a marathon sad. I feel the sadness of my next sixty birthdays. I can't ask for what I want because what I want isn't tangible. I feel guilty for wanting it. I'm trying to not care. To be cool. To be okay. It seems that the right thing, the noble thing, is to not care. And for that to work, other people have to care. But they don't. So I learn how to make myself smaller and smaller every year. I won't blow out candles. I'll just be easy.

SPRINGER

I'm trying to sleep but
I can't stop thinking about you
It could've been me
In some other life but
That would still include a loss
Just a different kind
My arms can only stretch so wide
And some things are
Simply not up to how
Much I can carry if what I want
Is intent on evading my grasp

The world can say no
After it's already said yes twice
You can try the open field
Or the cage and maybe
One is right but who knows
And it's too late anyway

So we get back in the car
And pick up donuts
And hug in the parking lot
And I suppose it is better
To be open than to
Never make the drive

I come home and
I am grateful for it
The warm breath on my ankles
The resolved hierarchy

We have said our piece
Shown our teeth and
Decided that we like
Having each other around
And I often forget to see
The miracle in that

I will keep trying
To offset wanting with
Loyalty to the current but
How I would have loved
To have been the one
To love you

V.

CRANBERRIES

I'm boiling water for tea to keep my eyes open. The midday dreams are tempting but I've flirted with enough of them to know how this ends. I figure I should start stealing glances at restraint for a change. Lean in toward the temperance so that it gets a peek down my shirt. I gasped when I saw the sudden yellow of the forsythia from a different angle. Both it and the rows of daffodils that line the sidewalks seem to have sprung up overnight. The earl grey was half gone when I came across a photo of two nuns holding up a puppy they'd just rescued from the shelter, and even with masks on, you could tell they were smiling. I thought of you again and how I missed you, and then I gave myself grief for loving the things I can't have the hardest. In the same way I go to call you and then realize I don't have your number. In the same way that I believe I would excuse all of your indiscretions if I could just sit and watch you read. In the same way I seem to always find the words more easily in the dark than with the lights on.

Maybe you don't know
how much room I have
made for you inside of me

INOSCULATION

There are squills scattered between new grass and brown leaves that don't know how to leave a party while it's still warm. I've passed through this lonely park this island pasture between channels of blacktop hundreds of times without noticing that the tree at the far edge is made up of two. One has cracked the other's broad trunk base and pushed itself up between obliging layers of bark peeled back like a pomelo. It shoots straight up the center like a splayed hand all subtle and proud of its intrusion. Or maybe it isn't aware that it has torn itself through the middle of something else. Maybe you don't know how much room I have made for you inside of me or that I am waiting for you to keep tearing me apart.

PASTIME

There's a line that keeps us on the edge of our seats but it only works if we never get greedy enough to cross it. We won't keep score forever but I haven't thought that far in advance anyway. It's a staring contest and I can't look away. If I can keep myself distracted with the peripherals then I won't have time to get bored of the elephant. The problem is, the deadwood always catches fire and I can't seem to stop feeding it the best of me.

SMALL TALK

When someone asks if you prefer summer or winter what they really mean is—I want to know, are you better at warming up or cooling off. Do you feel more like yourself beneath layers or lying out for the sun to swallow you. Do you run the shower too hot or do you sit on the stoop, cigarette glowing orange between your fingers, heart beating hard and slow. I want to know, when I lift up your shirt, will I see a stranger. I saw a dead bird on the sidewalk this morning and a man walking with a coffee mug in his left hand, talking to a neighbor, and I wondered if it meant something, or if I mean anything, to you.

I wonder how often
the things we call
our favorites were
really just within reach

SUGAR ANTS

Every morning, I wake up and wipe out a neat row of ants that stretches from the bathroom to the kitchen and appears overnight. At first, I felt sorry but soon realized that I can talk myself into coolness if the line grows thick enough. How easily I become a heavy fist, a spiteful thumb. How quickly a life can shift from precious to afflicting. Today I learned that my sugar ants like the taste of honeycomb and dates the best. Or maybe those were the only things they could find a way into.

I wonder how often the things we call our favorites were really just within reach.

i miss you even though
i won't talk to you

BOYS DON'T CRY

The daffodils have come and gone
The dandelions keep losing parts of themselves
Which is something I understand
No matter how far I run up the hill
I am always at the bottom of another one
And I miss you even though I won't talk to you
I listen to the music you showed me when I was a kid
And I cry a little on your birthday even though I hate you
And it would be easier if you were a memory
That I could childishly embellish
I know it's fucked up but it's your fault
That I'll only forgive you when you're gone
And you're not here to tell me
That you don't need my forgiveness

It felt better
to imagine
there was more
than there was

STICKY

We used to bite the green tips
Off dozens of honeysuckles
And with tiny fingernails
Drag out their white stems
As thin as a snagged thread
In the hem of our plaid jumpers
We took turns sticking out our tongues
For a drop of nectar
Every so often I pinched the ends
Pulled too hard and nothing gave
But I would still put my lips to it
To make sure that
I wasn't missing something
These days I wonder if
I wanted to taste it so badly
That it felt better to imagine
There was more than there was
It was in these intrusive vines
I learned a secret could be
As sweet as I wanted it to be
Given that I met with hidden delights
Just a little at a time
It feels like wearing a different flesh
To be so unafraid of leaning in for a kiss
Then tossing the flowers at my feet
Oblivious to my hand in their wilt

maybe I am
looking for you
in everyone
I meet

FIG LEAF

When you crack the door
I fling it wide open
Maybe I think we get along
Better than anyone
Who really knows me
Maybe that is a lazy elusion
Side-stepping the truth
Because as soon as I feel
Your arms around my waist
I pull away looking
For new ways to
Fall into someone else
But I still meet you there
In the grave of closeness
Maybe I am looking for you
In everyone I meet
The world keeps throwing
Us together and I let it

i turn my aching
into poems
that you don't know exist

FIFTEEN

I'm getting better at writing laments
Without the need to send them
Instead, I turn my aching into poems
That you don't know exist
Or maybe, someday, they'll be inside a book
On a shelf somewhere
And you'll pick it up and flip through
And just miss it
The page that is a silent scream
The page that spells out your name
In covert letters
The page that is still fifteen

PINK FROSTING

There are two types of love
That isn't true, there are infinite
But for the sake of this feeling
I will pretend there are just two
There is just me and you
But that isn't true either
Anyway, there is the love that wakes
Me up in the middle of the night
And the love that holds me until
I fall back asleep—is it greedy
To want you to be both

EMBER

Am I eternally damned
To forever be who I was

How much space do I need
To get between us to
Become a different person
Someone you would not
Recognize between aisles
At the grocery store
Walking up to me
Introducing yourself
Saying, "you look so
Familiar, but I just can't
Place it."

I dream of burying myself
Deep within myself
Like a time capsule in the
Backyard that I forgot
About but maybe
Someone someday
Will remember

I am painfully separate
from the world of others

CEASING

There are stray moments
When I am sitting next to
An open window in the late afternoon
Or when I first step into the backyard
And notice the smell of heat and grass
That I am ageless — that time is a stranger
I have forgotten what day it is
Or that I am painfully separate
From the world of others
The man walking down the sidewalk
Looking at his own feet
The father I no longer know
Or that, one day, I will have to
Grow up for good
It is in these secret meetings
That I find you
Without the flush of guilt
The memory of a feeling
Sitting on the sill
Taunting me to pick it up

IN THE PINES

There is a world I haven't given myself to
I feel resistant to the passage of time
I can't stop thinking about the forest
About disappearing in it
When the sun retreats I'll get lost in its deep green
And the moonlight will follow me
As I trip over the roots of the pines I ache to climb
I peer up at their branches—I cannot reach them
They cannot hold me
But I picture myself hidden there
Reposed with a book in my hand
Tangled in the foliage, dripping with the sap of giving in
The shadows enveloping us
The ground moving further away
Until I am too afraid to look down
And I wait for you   to look up

THE WEATHERMAN

I tie tiny bells to myself
As though I am fashioning a wind chime
Out of defiant and impulsive limbs
Tying myself up with good intentions
So that I might hear when the world begins
To move through me too quickly
Or in the wrong direction
I don't allow my fingers to grasp
What they as a small child
Would have picked up without thought
I imagine myself as a butterfly
With an inch of fishing line
Fastened between pert wings
I am still but I am not thoughtless
I dream of lefty scissors and
Falling objects with sharp edges and
Cupped hands that will
Lift me into the air and show me that
The sky is just as much mine
As it is yours

i have always
been familiar with
the weight of wanting
to disappear

MELT

I used to feel small when hurt but now there is fire in my ache. The anger is a fist made of fingers that once used to cover my face. I have always been familiar with the weight of wanting to disappear but now the heat cuts through me and I find myself screaming inside of myself. The scream is mostly a question, to which silence answers that I must habituate to your lack of reason. I am a flame charring the wick of a candle that does not remember my name.

CRUEL SUMMER

It's the second week of August. Are you dreading the end.
Its bare shoulders and laze and remembering your body.
Or are you, like me, tired of the glare. Waiting for a storm.
Eager for the days to grow shorter, the sharpness of a blue
morning, something like a beginning. The too early piles
of brown leaves remind me that it is easier to pine, to ache,
than to sit in the current of the sun as it washes over my
longing. It swells while I look the other way.

SEEING A CROW IN A DREAM

The poem I resist digs deeper into my chest like a buried soulmate. It grows blurry and distant until I can't find the sharpness of it, but I can still taste how it made me feel. The feeling becomes a dull hunger. The distorted memory of a bite. Still gnawing, lost, hopeful that I will give in to my undoing and gruesomely reveal the bloodied shadow of a bluff that has been called home. Neither of us can sleep. My teeth ache. When the sky turns purple with torment, I end up in the woods collecting feathers, consumed in the uncaging of a fire that will never catch.

MOST DAYS
I CANNOT GET
MYSELF TO BE
A REAL PERSON

FOR THE BEST

I want you to see me on my knees
Scrubbing the bathroom tile
I want you to know that
I am much worse up close
I am the honeyvine growing
Around the white fence post
I am sleeping in again
Flush faced and pathetic
Saliva on the pillowcase
Knot of hair in the shower drain
I am slouching on the park bench
Shaking in the parking lot
And when I eat blueberries
My entire mouth gets
Stained purple like a little kid
Most days I cannot get myself
To be a real person — I exist
In an expanse that becomes
Embarrassing when revealed
That I do not deserve it
That I am more luck than sweat
This dull waste of freedom
Enclosed in a lingering bruise
A self-wrecking that I can't
Seem to quit

by the middle
of the week,
I am tired
of being a person

INTANGIBLE

By the middle of the week, I am tired of being a person. So on Thursdays, give me space to die a little in private. I don't want to go to the grocery store, fold laundry, wash a pan, or cut up artichokes for a salad. Let me sit quietly in a room alone with my knees folded to one side. I will retreat into myself, where I have resided obscurely through immeasurable and contrasting lives, all disorganized and stacked on top of each other in the pit of my stomach. Sometimes, they spill out of my mouth like sheets of ice because of you and your nagging fingers pulling at my bottom lip, hungry for me to tell you what I think before I know how to say it.

sometimes I feel so full
of tenderness that I am
convinced I could live a
hundred lifetimes carrying
the same heart in my chest
and it still wouldn't be enough

FIND ME

Quiet flashes of lightning through the blinds tint my room faint blue and for a fleeting moment I am glowing. Sometimes I feel so full of tenderness that I am convinced I could live a hundred lifetimes carrying the same heart in my chest and it still wouldn't be enough. Take my hand in yours, press the inside of my wrist to your cheek, bite down if you need to. The soft rain on the window is a harvest. I tell the moon that I am not afraid to lie down in the morning grass and it has no choice but to take my word for it. I want to believe that I am more than a pulse. That you could love the shadow of something. That you could feel your way through the dark, knowing somehow that my palms are reaching back.

VI.

DAGGER

I seem to like the odds better when they're stacked against me. I have always been terrified of bee stings. I count down the days until spring but forget that going outside means exposing my bare stomach to venom. Everything is a trade. A kiss is pointless without a little teeth. Recently I learned that the odds are six million to one and now I can't stop thinking about how romantic it would be to be the one. How it would feel to get close enough to make you flinch. Is it possible that the burn is worth the thrill. You chose me over everyone else with stickier hands. Isn't that all I've ever wanted.

BURIED

It's a race with the blade
Of who can sink faster
But my heart doesn't
Know what's good for it
So I take the stairs
Two at a time and
Search for my grave
At the top

Tell me that I don't
Have to carve my name
Into the granite
That I could
Leave the bottom
Of this page blank
And you would
Fill in the rest

NIGHTMARE

Where were you when
The branches were scraping my window
When I was staring out at the cul-de-sac
Clutching the landline to my chest
Once I thought I saw a bear in the woods
Across from the bus stop but it turned out
To be just a pile of tangled brush
You know I still see things in the dark
The other night I woke up from a bad dream
And saw teeth that weren't there
I managed to blink them away but
There are some things that I can't
Like the shadow in the doorway that
Visits most nights and the open hand
That I am doing everything not to grab
It pretends that it needs me but
Really it's the other way around

sometimes,
the heaviness feels
a lot like being held

CRUSH ME

When I'm older, I'll give more of myself to the yellow morning. By then, I'll have a front porch where the honeybees join me for breakfast, and I won't worry about the sting any longer than I should, and the day will be enough. But for now, I am still waiting for a flood, still waist-deep in the rain. I am taking communion with the things that hurt, letting them melt on my tongue like hot wax. The broken clock, and the hollow haunting, and the song that says what I can't. I think the winter knows me better than I'd like to admit. But sometimes, the heaviness feels a lot like being held and so I let it crush me.

YOU GET ME

We're chewing the same glass
With closed mouths
Waking up every morning
At the bottom of the same hill
I want to tell you that it goes away
The burning pulse of a haunted vein
But I haven't been able to stop
Pressing my fingers into my wrist
Making sure that you're still there

PEN PAL

I want you to know me by my handwriting
Let's start licking envelopes just to say hello
I'll sit at my desk drinking coffee in the morning
A stack of letters in the drawer tied up with string
You know I would keep every single one of yours
Even if you lived next door. Even if you wrote everyday
I don't know how to throw anything away

I look down and
my shadow is there.
I don't know who
I am without it.

DON'T BE A STRANGER

This afternoon, I went to the office supply store with my little brother. We were buying markers and glitter glue and I was someone whose hands didn't tremble. I was someone who didn't want to go home. When I am driving with the radio on, I am an actor in a bad movie. When I am picking up scallions at the grocery store, I am the girl you believe in. But when I'm agonizing, when I'm breaking, when I'm alone—I look down and my shadow is there. I don't know who I am without it.

The first thing
I do when I wake
up is fall apart

FLOOD WATCH

I peel the Band-Aid slowly and give myself to the cruelty in parting. What could have been a wince becomes a tedious affair with tenderness. I am breaking my legs performing for no one, hoping that with enough practice, I may become better at being wrecked. The first thing I do when I wake up is fall apart. If I loved myself better, I would stand further from the window when it storms. But I don't. I fall asleep in the shower. I wash the dishes and burn the toast. I crack the door to smell the rain. I wait for you to let yourself in.

I want to hear the poems
you would write if you
knew no one would read them

JUST BETWEEN US

I want to get you alone. I want to know what you listen to while driving down the quiet dark of an empty road. I want to follow you around the grocery store, stepping slowly through a Sunday afternoon. I want to hear the poems you would write if you knew no one would read them. The ink smeared, letters leaning forward a bit like you couldn't get them down fast enough. I want to hear you say you're not ready to leave yet. The moon is full and low, and everything is how you pictured it would be, back when the world felt small. Now it's glowing at the edges, swelling into something so wide that your heart can hardly wrap itself around all of the imminent lightness. This is what you've been waiting for, and you are laughing so hard that you cover your face with a modest hand. I want to tell you that you don't have to do that with me. So you take mine instead, and we start walking down the sidewalk, not knowing which direction is home.

HIDDEN VEIN

Not today
There's not enough
Sun in my blood
To do what
I'm supposed to

Can you make sense
Of the silence
Can you make the bed
Can you carry the sadness
So I don't have to

FRESHWATER

The pearl gets lost
In the mouth of
What should have been
It's never in my palm
Never strung on a
Silk thread clasped
Around my neck
That I fiddle with while
Waiting to buy
A carton of strawberries
Can't I find it in the fleeting
On your tongue
Beneath my pillow
While I fall asleep
All I can think about
When I'm driving
In the rain is that
It'd be nice to have someone
To call—that I would be
Different and somehow
That is better

you taught me that
the future is someone
i'd like to meet

C.L.

Leave your blue shadow at the door. This quiet house is more bear hug than birdcage. In December we'll put up string lights and wear thick socks by the fireplace. A pie baking in the oven turning the air into clove perfume. I can't remember where the trees begin but I hope they are covered in snow and that we can see them from the window. Maybe in the morning while we're drinking coffee and frying eggs. I imagine one day I'll wake up and forget where I am for a moment and when I remember I will curl back into the pillow knowing life can be more dream than nightmare. You pulled the curtains aside when I asked for five more minutes. The sunlight painted my sleepy limbs before I knew I was ready. You taught me that the future is someone I'd like to meet.

CHOKE

You don't know and I can't tell you
So you'll go on not knowing
And I'll go on feeling like
I'm trapped inside of myself

COMFORT ZONE

I am afraid I feel most like myself alone
with my daydreams because that was
how I survived my teenage years. But I'm
twenty-five now, and there is no one left
to hide from. So why do I still feel like
hiding? Why am I better at existing in
my head—and yours—than in a body?

I thought
by now
I would have
what I want

OUT OF THE BLUE

The first of April means I have made it
The trees are budding purple flowers
The sun sticks around for dinner

I thought I did a good job letting go this winter
I kept my back turned to the stove
I did my best to forget
About walking out of the door without a coat on

I thought by now I would have what I want
It doesn't matter—I have yet to meet a spring that hurries
Toward me like a lover at baggage claim
A March that doesn't drag its feet through the frost

whatever you want

FULL

It is a miracle that anyone
Left waiting at the dinner table
With their plate licked clean
Even the salmon skin
Even the broccoli stalks
Were not slipped to the dog
Finds themselves, one day
Far beyond the memory of
Falling asleep on empty stomachs
In the kitchen, whisking together
Eggs, milk, and vanilla
While the stove heats up
Sprinkling cinnamon, nutmeg
And sugar over thick slices
Of brioche before
Browning them in a pan
Insisting that you help yourself
To seconds and thirds
That you bring some home with you
In borrowed Tupperware
Don't worry about returning it
Take whatever you want

IF I NEVER GOT OUT OF BED

Then I'd never know
the relief of crawling back
into it again

TWO LIVES

I want two lives. One in the middle of nowhere, where it gets really quiet, the kind of quiet you forget exists, and when you look up at night, you can see the stars dusted across the sky like a thousand glowing freckles. The other is in the middle of it all, where I am never alone, where there is always someplace open to buy a soda when I can't sleep, and the buzz of excess becomes as soothing as crickets chirping in the grass at dusk. In each life, there is a window I gaze out of, biting my nails, longing for the next.

I have found that
if I do not have
tomorrow, I cannot
seem to face today

TOMORROW TOMORROW TOMORROW TODAY

Tomorrow
I will get out of bed and stretch in the sunlight
I will walk the dog slowly so that he can sniff
All the patches of grass that he likes
Tomorrow
I will make blueberry muffins
Or peanut butter banana bars and
The kitchen will smell warm, like spring
I will write with the window open
I will find my words before lunch so that
I am not left searching for them in the dark
Instead I will drink lemon ginger tea
And listen to the heavy rain in bed
And muse about what lies ahead because
I have found that if I do not have
Tomorrow
I cannot seem to face
Today

I AM STILL LEARNING
HOW TO CARRY MYSELF

BAD AT EXISTING

I have not always felt like a stranger. There were years when I did not even think of myself, just the smell of squished fruit on the sidewalk fallen from the towering Ginkgo Biloba trees. I remember her in flashes. In the mist rising over a wet field in western Maryland in late December, heaps of leaves walked over until they were dust. I played Uno on my neighbor's front porch and looked for blue-eyed cicadas in the backyard. Sometimes, we would walk to get soft serve before sunset, and it seemed summer would go on forever. The moon followed me in the backseat of my parent's car until I fell asleep and woke up in my bed the next day. I try not to think about the last time this happened or how I did not know it would be the last time. I am still learning how to carry myself.

Coda

LULLABY

I can't be okay if you're not okay. I can't sleep if I know you're awake. So I'll stay awake too. I'll be tired in the morning. I'll show you that I was there even if only in my dark circles. In my chewed lip. I was there. It didn't matter. You're tired too. I can't save you. It's not fair.

I KNOW THE END

I am so good at time travel
I go to the grocery store
On a Tuesday morning and
Listen to music while picking
Out coffee creamer
And I swear it's 2008
Everything is much smaller
And quieter and safer
And I'm just a normal girl
In the express checkout line
And nothing is scary
Because it has already happened

ANOTHER LIFE

Today was good / And when I think about why / It is so glaringly obvious that I am still a little kid / The smallest things make me glow / Sunlight and coffee and a breakfast sandwich / My sister / Unexpected ease / A two-mile walk with the dog at sunset / It was all so normal and relatively insignificant / But I suppose that's what I crave / I suppose what was most glaring was my joy in the absence of torment / Could there really be a life made up by one after the other of these / Where the trudge is an off day rather than the marrow / I cannot fathom that kind of happiness / I cannot believe some get to be so free

i remember
who i am

COMPASS HEART

The forest of being
Is thick with green ceilings and
Densely pebbled paths
Sometimes the downpour cannot
Reach me and the trodden dirt
Becomes like a second skin
I lean over a pool of old rainwater
Clouded with unanswered questions
And I cannot find myself in it
But then I catch a ray of sunlight
Between two holy branches
And it melts away the fog of doubt
The sky reveals itself to me and
I remember who I am
My roots dig deeper
Into the warm earth even when
I cannot watch them grow
And with each new step
I realize that I do not need a map
To know which way to go

MUSE

When I can't find the words
Will you place them on my tongue
And let me pretend that
They're mine
I keep spending more time
With the moon than I should
But it's the one thing
That reminds me of my pulse
Every night is longer than the last
I fall asleep hoping that
You might come to me in a dream
So that by the time I wake up
I will have found something to say

UNFORGETTABLE

I don't write for weeks
And then I do
And it feels like taking a bite out of a piece of fruit
That will never spoil
No matter how long it sits on the counter
Forgotten
I can always pick it back up again
It will always be sweet

BUT THERE IS
NOTHING BEAUTIFUL
ABOUT THE WAY
THAT I BREAK

AMULET

I would rip my heart from my chest and place it in your hands if it meant you could feel what I feel. The truth is that this isn't much different. The opening up and the coming apart. The blood beneath my fingernails. In the dark, I wish I was the girl in your head—sunlight reaching for you after the rain. Soft grey morning turned pink. But there is nothing beautiful about the way that I break. Would you pick up the pieces. Would you put them in your pocket. Would you carry me around.

i feel the end
of the world
on the tip
of my tongue

SAVING MYSELF

I am all broken skin and soft stomach
Lungs that have forgotten how to be full
I panic in public restrooms
My heart lives in my throat
And I am very nervous
Very terrified
Very human
Yet, I still take myself out
Still sit in the thick air
Although the air at home feels
Much easier to breathe
I feel the panic
I feel the end of the world
On the tip of my tongue
And I live. I move. I continue.

I have always dreamed of being rescued
I never realized
I've been rescuing myself
This whole time

DIRT ROADS

If I were to press my palms on the jagged edge of my fear
With the soles of my bare feet parallel to the sky
And sun-bleached hair spreading out over the grass
Like a picnic blanket for little bugs in the dirt
To sit upon and eat finger sandwich crumbs
I could focus my gaze on the upside-down sea
And watch all the things I carry float around
In the blue-black waves
Wiggling like half hardened Jell-O
Where the small fish nor the white sharks
Give a damn whether I am beautiful or witty
Or doing okay

And when the sky fades as it always does
And the tide continues to pirouette
In her borrowed pink ballet shoes
With moon dust in the binding

I will keep running down dirt roads
Until my lungs burn
Until the headwind feels like home

GOOD ENOUGH

There is a place in between
Where the water glistens at dusk
Where the birds are falling asleep
With worms in their bellies
Where the sand is soft and warm
Where the sea is calling you

And I will wait there on the shore
While you shed the heaviness
Of holding up the world
While you dance naked
In the moonlight
While you let the waves
Wash over you

There is time to heal

To be free
And easy
And human

To be light expanding
Over the haze

I am sorry
I don't always
see you but
I promise that
I want to

THIRTY

Today is your birthday so I made you a card
That says Happy Monday
When you get home from work I will light a candle
In the bathroom
And put on your music so you can shower while
I put hot water on the stove for macaroni and cheese
Because that is the best way I know how to love you

Sometimes you still feel like a stranger
And I wonder how that's possible
That I could know someone so well
And in some ways not at all
I want to spend the rest of my life making a list
Of the things that you like
So that I can stop guessing—so that knowing you
Is like knowing myself
I am sorry I don't always see you but I promise
That I want to

it's sad to see
anything torn apart

A WEDNESDAY IN APRIL

I was sitting on a splintering wooden bench in the middle of town next to the old hardware store when I saw the most darling Shih Tzu hanging out the driver's side window in a car stopped at the traffic light. His owner was beaming and kissing his little head. They looked so happy together, and it made me smile.

I read a poem today where Mary Oliver refers to the beauty of the world and asks, "what else is it for?" (other than to bring us peace and comfort.) I like that idea. That nature and animals are here to show us what love looks like. To be there for us when the world is overwhelming and scary. But then I think of tornadoes and grizzly bears and wonder—bears look cute from afar, rolling around alone in a giant field of flowers, but the salmon would disagree. Tornadoes are kind of beautiful when there are no living things in their paths. But there always are. Even if they aren't human. Even if they're just trees. It's sad to see anything torn apart.

YOU ARE MORE
THAN ENOUGH

THE MOM FRIEND

You are freshly baked sourdough bread
Torn into as many pieces as there are plates

A wood burning stove
On cold December mornings

A soft hand to hold
A quiet understanding

You are the person that others
Come home to

I hope that you remember
To pour yourself a cup of tea

To lay down in some soft meadow
To let the butterflies play with your hair

While you listen to the heartbeat of the earth
As it whispers that you are more than enough

You do not have to earn
What you so generously give

i will love you
in the shadows

GOLDEN

I will love you
With paint in your hair

I will love you
With your magnum opus
Hanging in the Louvre

When the crowd
Is on its feet

When the curtains close

I will love you
In the shadows

Where the sun
Cannot find you
Where you are the sun

When all the leaves
Have fallen from
Their branches

When all that is left
Is the way
Your eyes light up
At the sight of
Fallen snow

SEEN

This morning, I went
out and bought a
bouquet of foil balloons.
I stopped by the
market and paid the
baker to ice a
cake just for you.
While you were still
asleep, I hung streamers
from the ceiling. I
invited over all of
our friends. I sat
by your bed and
kissed your forehead. I
told you that it
was the beginning of
everything. You smiled and
hid your face because
you thought I'd forgotten.
We emerged from the
dark room. You did
not wish you were
someplace else. You were
there. I watched as
the heaviness left you.
As you floated up
to the ceiling. When
it was over, you
went back to your
room and shut the

door. The next day,
while making lemon ricotta
pancakes in the kitchen,
you asked me to
keep the streamers up.
You wanted to remember.

THE SCIENTIST

When every rock
Has been turned over
When you have asked
Every question
When the tangled thread
Of this corner of the universe
Is straightened out
And sewn into your collar
We will set off fireworks
In the backyard
We will book a trip
To fly across the world
And swim as deeply
As our lungs will allow
In an unknown ocean
Where at the bottom
The blue seaweed sways
And the pearls
You will string together
To hang around my neck
Sit inside buried clams

PICK UP THE PEN

Do not be afraid of the wide open spaces
The night sky above the city that echoes silence
That begs for you to fill it with stars

You are so used to seeing a blank page
As something empty that
You have forgotten your fullness
All the words and worlds that live inside you
That do not make their way to the surface

You have spent your whole life
Walking down cleared paths
Rather than paving your own

But now, it's your turn
To write something new

THE WINDOW SEAT

All the mountains left to climb will be there tomorrow
Their peaks dusted in gold waiting
For your footprints to kick up wonder in your wake
And when you make it to the top
As the sun begins to lower itself
Over the edge of the world
Turning everything orange
You will breathe in the sunset
And carry it with you wherever you go

FREE

You are strength that stretches across unbending bones
Bones that have kept themselves intact
Despite the weight of elephants
And when you fall, you do not crumble
You do not count the blades
Of grass in front of your nose
You see the sky hanging over your head like a bedsheet
Something you can press your hand into
Something you can pull down
When you are ready to start over
You will get out of bed
Pull on your socks
Lace up your shoes
And take the first step toward
Something better

9 IN THE MORNING

You wake up
and open the curtains.
Music from your bedroom
softly wafts into the kitchen
where you are making coffee
and scrambling eggs and
cutting up a piece of fruit.
The weather is mild so you
sit outside and listen to
The birds sing. When it begins
to rain, the birds become quiet
and take cover in the bushes,
but you stay put and listen
to the rain song. You notice that
it sounds a lot like hope.
And when you go inside to
do the dishes, your mother
calls and asks if she can come
over to borrow a mop. She left
the window open during
the storm. She doesn't have
a key so you will need to be
there to let her in. You say okay.
You don't mind. You didn't have
much planned for the day, anyway.

The End

Acknowledgments

This book could have easily never existed. Yet, it exists–entirely because of the extraordinary people in my life: my friends, family, and especially you, my readers.

In 2020, three publishers decided to pass on this collection. I felt like I had failed. I was shattered. I asked myself, cloaked in shame, *"where do I go from here?"*

First, it was the thought of my readers that lifted me from that dark place. I knew I had to get my words to you somehow–even if it meant setting aside my pride and returning to my roots in self-publishing. It felt like going backwards at first, but the road is never as straightforward as we imagine it will be, and through what seemed like a loss, I discovered the beauty in paving my own way.

The irony is that in retaking this self-publishing journey, just like in 2015 when I released my first book, *Eighteen Years*, I became more connected with my love of writing than ever. I uncovered a reinvigorated sense of passion for poetry and the all-consuming and exhilarating task of creating a book from scratch.

Then it was my husband, Christopher, who dusted me off. He has always believed in me more than I believe in myself. He continually reminds me of the importance of doing everything from a place of strength rather than fear. After three rejections, my morale was low. I felt desperate to find anyone to publish this book. I was looking for someone to tell me that I was good enough. Christopher inspired me to take a different approach. Because of him, I felt empowered enough to take ownership of this book and make it something I was proud of. I am deeply grateful for how he always motivates me to do what feels right rather than simply taking the path of least resistance.

While writing *Bad At Existing*, I became acquainted with the invaluable nourishment of connecting with fellow writers. F.S. Yousaf, the author of *Sincerely,* played a significant role in the creation of this book. He was there reading my poems, offering advice and reassurance every step of the way. I believe the world would be better if everyone had a friend like Farhan.

I am deeply grateful for Rupi Kaur's friendship and kindness, which has felt much like a life raft. In the depths of my discouragement, I found solace in Rupi's words of encouragement. She is the kind of person who makes you feel seen. I know many of you know what I mean. Tumblr girls, always and forever.

The internet is a weird place that does wonderful things every once in a while, like connecting me with Leah Lu, who designed the cover of *Bad At Existing*. Leah illustrated my second book, *Please Don't Go Before I Get Better*, back in 2018, and she was the first person I thought to design the cover of this book. She has impeccable taste and talent and is also one of the best people I know. She gets it, you know? Everyone judges a book by its cover. The cover Leah created for *Bad At Existing* made me believe in love at first sight. I'm so glad I got the opportunity to work with her again and will be singing her praises forever and ever.

And a few more words about you. I started writing poetry and posting it on my blog when I was sixteen. I'm not sure I would be here today–nearly a thousand poems later–if it weren't for you. You found me, took my hand, and said, *"I feel this too. You're not the only one."* That has made all of the difference.

Thank you for always seeing me when I've wanted to hide. Thank you for showing me that it is more gratifying to acknowledge that sometimes I'm bad at existing than pretending I have it all together.

Thank you for helping me see that it is better to show up messy and honest than to hide in detachment and the illusion of perfection. You have changed my life.

I am so glad you exist.

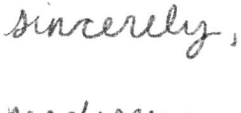

sincerely,

madisen

MADISEN KUHN is a poet from Charlottesville, Virginia. She likes to explore themes of identity, belonging, sexuality, and mental illness in her work. At nineteen, Madisen self-published her first collection of poetry, *Eighteen Years*. She went on to publish *Please Don't Go Before I Get Better* in 2018 with Gallery Books. Her third book, *Almost Home*, was a semi-finalist in the Goodreads Choice Awards—Best Poetry Books of 2019. Most mornings, she drinks coffee with her husband Christopher, surrounded by their three dogs, and is glad she exists.

Printed in Great Britain
by Amazon

12500670R00161